Published by Beadle Books
New York and London
2025

Copyright © 2025 Yunus Tuncel
Cover & Book Design: Oz Paker

ISBN: 978-0-9962058-7-0 (Paperback)
ISBN: 978-0-9962058-8-7 (Ebook)

Notebook R: Human Relations

Spirits Close, Paths Apart

Yunus Tuncel

New York

Bear that solitude a little longer...

Contents

Indeptedness and Preface 9

Fore-Thoughts from Phronistery 13

Experience in Relations 17

Living with Others 21

Relations and Emotions 27

Un/familiar Relations 37

Between the Familiar and the Unfamiliar 41

Techne, Technology and Relations 53

On Friendship 57

Sex in Relationships 63

Ancients and the Care for the Self and the Other 65

On Bondage in Human Relations: The Herd and the Control .. 69

On Ruling and Hierarchical Relations 71

Needs, Needs, and Needs 75

On Silence in Relations 77

Language in Relations 79

After-Thoughts on the Staircase 81

Last Stop on this Aphoristic Route 83

A Short Bibliography 87

Also by Yunus Tuncel 93

Indebtedness and Preface

I am indebted to all those whom I met over the years and who presented a plethora of character traits, whether good or bad, pleasant or unpleasant, or liberating or depressing. I learned much from what I observed in myself, others and my relations with them, humans and non-humans alike. No doubt, the biggest gratitude goes to all the aphorists, listed at the end of the book, who inspired me and others in the journey of our psychological observations. Aphorisms speak across cultures and generations; I hope these aphorisms find such echo in the readers of this book.

I am thankful to the cats I live with, Kara, Milo and Miso, who showed me another way of being-in-the-world and helped me improve my relations with others, human or non-human. I wish I could explain to them all of these philosophical concepts and insights and show my appreciation to them in human terms, but they will find them too boring. As from the human community, I thank my friend and publisher for this book, David Kilpatrick, who has always supported me in my struggles as a thinker and a writer. Next thank you note goes to the book designer, Oz Paker, who gave her grace and taste of design to this book. Many thanks are due to my friend, Luke Trusso, who read my manuscript and did not spare any of his editorial comments, even if they were harsh. Lastly, I appreciate the support and presence of Meltem and Mayra and many friends who have been companions on this difficult but joyful life's journey and for testing me on the difficulties of human relations.

Human relations are multi-layered and fraught with many complexities most of which escape our attention in our daily hustle and bustle. Most simply live in an auto-pilot mode without heeding these intricacies and any attempt to work on broken parts of these relations. It takes at least two to do so and more than that it demands introspection and willingness to do so. Working on a relationship also means working on one's own self, which demands courage and solitude. Most humans do not have this type of courage or are not equipped to look at their own selves as a work of art to sculpt and transform.

The aphorisms in this book are fragments for the care of the self and the self's relations to others. Although the main thrust of the book is on human relations, one must also consider relations holistically and reflect on how the nature of human relations bear on one's relations to all beings, not just humans.

Fore-Thoughts from Phronistery

1

Types relate to each other according to their archetypical traits and tendencies, which often lie in the background.

2

One must be measured in society, according to the affects he produces; all else is a burden on that society.

3

More often than not, in intimate relations it is not what one does, but rather what one does not do, that is most hurtful.

4

Humans often judge others through their silence.

5

To expect a relationship without conflict is to desire to have a trophy without toil.

6

When a relationship becomes nocent, there is no innocence left on any side.

7

Prospicience is needed to minimize conflicts in human relations.

8

Pervicacious and inflexible types make relations difficult and static.

9

Controlling others is often couched in care for others.

10

If one treats children like dependent idiots, they could turn out to be so in their adulthood.

11

How one relates to one part of Being is reflective of how one relates to the whole Being, or vice versa.

12

On-going troubled relations, which nonetheless remain intimate, pain us like nails pierced in the flesh.

13

For human relations to work, diverse needs of all parties in the relationship must be aligned.

14

Human relation is not a mathematical formula, because you cannot draw a straight line from Person A to Person B.

15

The Zenzic in Human Interactions! Both the positives and the negatives can multiply themselves in human relations. The former is less felt than the latter, especially when one side in the relation takes the other for granted, does not recognize the positives and is insensitive to the decline when one is blind to the negatives.

16

"Facts" and the obsession with facts common in the modern age and its news culture diminish the capacity to think and prevent humans from creating a healthy phronistery for themselves.

17

Humans, even if they are intimate, are never transparent or fully communicable to each other. Inner states reveal signs that are beyond ordinary communication. Thus remain humans to be black boxes to be deciphered.

18

Every human relation, intimate or not, flourishes in its own environment, taking root in the varieties of human institutions.

19

There are protean and rigid natures; both types may be problems in human relations. The former easily adapts to the circumstances at hand, where they should not adapt. On the other hand, the rigid person never bends and thereby misses the possibility of a rich experience.

Experience in Relations

20

Characters become enriched through lived experiences; however, the amount of experience one can have in one's life span is limited. It is, therefore, necessary to plunge into some of the fields of experience so as to live them fully and vigorously and to have a more wholesome experience, while some other fields will have to remain surface experience.

21

The Futility of Domination! In marriage relations where one side is dominant, as the male in patriarchal relations (but this can be extended to different types of family relations), children may not benefit from the good qualities of the suppressed side and would be left only with the negative qualities of the dominant side.

22

Compensatory Traits-Missing!!! When one does not know a person very well, whose vexing traits stand out like a thorny bush, one cannot know that person's amiable qualities which can offset those thorny qualities. Hence a poor judgment of that person arises…

23

How faults are managed is the crucible of every human relation. It is the mark of greatness to know one's faults; however, it makes one small when one denies or covers up one's faults.

24

When La Rochefoucauld writes: "Blemishes in the soul are like wounds on the body: no matter how skillfully they be healed, the scar will yet remain: and such a scar is liable to reopen at any moment." (Maxims 194). He makes a good point about the repetition of deep psychic wounds. This is why those who know their blemishes have to work around them so that they do not become sore spots in their relations with others.

25

The Golden Mean! Pessimists always focus on the awful, wretched conditions in humans and their relations, while optimists mostly on their good and shiny aspects. There must be a golden mean in-between, which perceives all colors, all modes of relations without prejudging them.

26

Both surface and depth experiences are equally necessary in different contexts of relations. One cannot avoid being superficial in public with those whom one hardly knows but yet has to interact with socially. However, one shall avoid being superficial in one's own field of activity.

Living with Others

27

As long as one lives with others, one must have social skills and should learn and know how to relate to different types of beings, especially those who are unlike one's own type of personality. On the other hand, regardless of one's sociability, one needs to always enjoy one's own solitude. It is in silent, meditative suffering that one cultivates one's self.

28

Depravity in Body. A hidden contempt for his body and the human body in general lies in Pascal's condemnation of 'diversion' in his *Pensées*. He thinks that such activities as dancing and sport, which he calls 'vain,' are distractions which take humans away from their more important goals and ideals, forgetting that such collective physical activities bring people together and contribute to individual and communal social being. Pascal also forgets that these physical cultural activities could also be goals to attain, but his faith prevents him from seeing it.

29

The self, whether real or illusory, is not a unitarian whole but a field of conflicting forces on lateral and vertical dimensions.

A person rich in the resources of character knows which part of that self to bring to foreground in relation with others.

30

Empathy is a bridge to others, which come from the resources of one's character, and such bridges come in different shapes and sizes. There are weak and strong, or shallow and deep bridges of empathy.

31

Empathy and its expression work at different levels and there are many reasons as to why some humans either seem not to be emphatic, even if they may be, and some others do not show empathy when it is needed, because they are unable.

32

It is best to contain one's protruding and disturbing pathologies within one's own self so as to sustain healthy human relations. For that, self-knowledge and self-care are necessary, not to mention empathy which enables us to understand what in us may be disturbing to others. Knowledge and care of the self help us find solutions and remedies.

33

In order to develop and sustain 'healthy' relationships, one must know one's authentic needs and learn to respect the needs of others. This basic insight, however, becomes less applicable when it concerns upbringing and education where children may not know their authentic needs.

34

The Pitfall of Care! In caring for others, one must truly suspend one's own interest, if that is possible, for that care not to turn into a control scheme.

35

Dangerous Emotions! Altruism and pity are the emotions that underlie the exercise of power over the other. Both hide behind the presumption of care for the other.

36

Thorny Bumps. When a defect or a character deficiency appears in one side in an intimate relationship, like love relation or friendship, a distance or an alienation could be felt on the other side, with no return to former intimacy.

37

Vexation, Irritation and End of Relations. Every human has their own unique dislikes and based on these dislikes a unique "coefficient of irritability." The end of relations, whether marriage, love or friendship, can be explained through this phenomenon of irritability and its co-efficiency. First, those who enter into relations do not know exactly what irritates the other person. As relations advance, these irritating elements come to the foreground. Second, as they get older, they may develop new 'irritating' habits or the old ones may become more irritating, and partners may have little or no tolerance for these habits. Lastly, the "coefficient of endurance" must be added to this subject to make the equation complete. Can one endure those irritating traits that exude from one's companions? The answer to this question will determine the longevity of the relationship.

38

The Banality of Relations! For monogamous relations to be erotic and exciting, partners must be open to extra-ordinary experiences and fulfill extra-ordinary acts. In this way, couples may save the relation from being dull and banal.

39

One must be willing to die in losing oneself in extraordinary acts.

40

In long-term relations, a chiasma between the two sides emerge as fusion takes roots in their persons, often unbeknownst to them. This phenomenon, a result of cohabitation, may be explained by way of shared climate, habitat, diet and rituals.

41

Close relationships that are stagnant, perpetuate character deficiency, or do not promote personal growth must be dissolved, if one wants to care for one's self.

42

Allegro vs. Andante! Unlike music, it is not advisable or desirable to bring slow and fast paced people together in close proximity. Instead of compensating for one another, they may cancel each other out.

43

Institutions complicate and often exacerbate human relations, although this may not be the intent of their original constitution.

44

Humans, Intelligent Animals? The unintelligent animals have better relations with their habitat than intelligent animals; this says much about the human lot on earth!

Relations and Emotions

45

Human relations, especially those that are close, are shaped by emotive phenomena, often unbeknownst to those who are in these relations. They lie in wait like tigers ready to jump. When one of these emotive phenomena comes to surface, that is, becomes known to them, their relation starts changing.

46

Discomfort in Comfort. They think they are comforting you in your pain with a few kind words, when, in fact, their effect creates the opposite, because you have already set that pain aside and moved on. And now they are putting salt on an old, closed wound.

47

Epigenesis of Emotions. We inherit emotions from our families, which we do not know we have inherited. That is the extent of unconscious forces.

48

Self-love. What exactly does one love in one's own self? That is the significant question. The self is not a unitarian whole, but rather a chaotic mess of diverse forces. What in that chaos one loves, determines one's character.

49

The Truth of Dreams; Truths Turned Upside Down. Dreams tell the truth and nature of our relations to others. Only if we heed them! A certain type of rationality, however, denies the truthfulness of dreams; how untruthful that is!

50

Vanity in Proximity! Only those who are close to us may know our true vanities!

51

Attraction/Repulsion! Why are decent characters attracted to vain characters in intimate settings? Is it because they are fooled by what the vain claims to have but, in fact, does not have? Or, the streak of vanity with its pomposity has a charm that attracts the decent one. "I cannot be that vain, but I can be with the vain and run on their glamorous vanity" may be the motto of the not so vain.

52

What kind of self is esteemed and how that self is formed in human relations remain central concerns for making of the self.

53

In every human relation, intimate or not, there remains a disparity of emotions felt by the different sides. Often such disparities are covered up and the pretension of having the same emotions comes to be accepted.

54

Unwanted Emotions! We are often faced with feeling, or pretending to feel, unwanted emotions. Someone next to us shows empathy to the loss of someone else in the group, but you yourself do not feel that empathy and yet are under social pressure to feel and show it. So, you end up feigning empathy, which you truly do not feel. And if the first person were also feigning it, you are feigning a feigned emotion, which is, a pretention of pretention. Such is human life, full of dissimulations! Philosophers have always sought remedy for such dissimulations but in vain! They found it in being enlightened, in being one's authentic self, in being faithful, in being truthful, in upholding ideas and ideals, in following the moral law, in being overhuman, and so on. Human being is an artifice of dissimulations and no remedy can cure that!

55

Dissemination and Discontentment! .—. The unhappiness of a person can spread faster and deeper in intimate relations than casual ones. This is not, however, to say that discontentment does not spread in strange waters.

56

Remedy for Contagious Discontentment? —.— When there is discontentment—and reasons are plenty to be so in today's world—an introspective person tries to remove it at its source so as not to make it chronic, or, in the absence of that, tries not make it a burden on others.

57

Discomfort from Within! Every human has a unique level of tolerance for discomfort and pain. Beyond the tolerable level one becomes disgruntled and cranky, which, if not contained, could impact relations adversely. The remedy for such situations is to be insightful about one's condition and not to let it enter into one's relation with others.

58

Discomfort from Without! The remedy for discomfort the origin of which lies in external factors is: a) to remove them,

b) to avoid them, c) to keep a physical and/or psychical distance to them, or, lastly, if none of these remedies work, d) to change one's self in such a way that what once caused discomfort is no longer a source of discomfort. The first two are for Epicureans and the last two for Stoics.

59

Who is Guilty? Those who are inclined to guilt are prone to easily pass judgment on others, because they are eager to seek and find someone guilty. The other way around holds true too: those who are quick to judge because they are righteous and believe to possess the truth are often guilt-ridden.

60

Guilt-seeking! The tendency to find someone guilty intensifies in proportion to what is at stake for the person who is looking for the guilty one. What may be at stake could be of a variety of issues: lover, job, reputation, life, freedom, etc.

61

The Unconscious Burden of Guilt. — Even if one tries to have a balance in one's life, one may not escape the hidden burden of being indebted to someone. This indebtedness could happen when someone does a favor to us and remembers it, while that favor falls into a hole of memory in us. An unexpected miscommunication or a non-communicated expectation ensues, while one side has no clue.

62

Guilt vs. Shame? There are rare moments in human relations when a dear friend keeps a secret from you so as to spare you the shame and prevent the contagion of guilt that may alienate you from society at large.

63

Human relations are sustained in a bundle of ever-changing emotions; when these emotions change, relations change, too!

64

The Truth of Emotions! Emotions felt and expressed in a relationship betray their nature.

65

Hierarchical relations are fraught with unspoken emotions which are more difficult to express than emotions in lateral relations.

66

The Heart at the Center! The heart, though not the only vital organ in the human body, has taken the center stage of human life and stands for many of its symbolism from love to war far more than any other organ; it is conceived as the "seat of emotions." The brain (or often referred to as the head) may be next in line. The liver or the kidney, however, do not come close; we do not say "I love you from the bottom of my kidney" and yet these and other organs are also vital for human life. Why this has been so can be explained not only by how amazing and complicated the organ of heart is but also by what it does, supply the living liquid of human and animal life: blood. Between two humans who are close, their hearts and bloods may not match physically, but they may be aligned symbolically and spiritually. Therefore, it is not so much the physicality of the heart but rather its symbolism that lies at the core of human relations.

67

Most intense emotions occur in affectivity, that is to say, someone or something invokes intense emotions in us, whether they are internal or external to us. Most emotions take on an object and that object can be another person. Someone makes us angry, envious, jealous or revengeful. More often than not, we cannot control our affects, even if we try to. The slightest thing one does may create a big impact on someone who is explosive. Affectivity is a closely-knit matrix and no one can see all the limbs and loose ends of the matrix. The Stoics could not understand this matrix; they believed one could control one's emotions. Emotions' affectivity, however, is not up to one individual, in whatever way that individual may have mastery over their emotions.

68

One often wonders how two humans who love each other deeply end up hating each other intensely. One asks, was it that they did not know each other very well when they declared their passionate love and some unpleasant qualities emerged as they got to know each other? Or, one of them changed radically, which pushed the changing side away from the other. Could it be that one lover did not find in the other what she was expecting from the relationship? Or, their values were already clashing when they met, but they could not be aware of it under the cloud of love? Could it be that other odious emotions such as envy and jealousy emerged, which eroded the emotion of love? "I cannot stand you because I envy you." Could that be written on the door of every decaying relationship?

69

Passions and Communities. Human collective living becomes more precious and enduring, when they are based on shared passions. This is why top to bottom arrangements and pre-determined social contracts often break down. This stems not only from suffering that ensues such impositions but also from the absence of common passions experienced by the community. The two may be related.

70

The Truth of Gossip! Although philosophers dislike gossip and dismiss it as 'doxa' or 'idle chatter,' it has a cathartic function in everyday life, similar to what psychotherapy aims to induce.

71

Disparity in Relations. Those who make immediate, superficial connections with each other based on their seeming identity will never understand the common bond that is formed among those based on their deep, authentic passions. Unfortunately, the former types of bond have been more prevalent than the latter in human society and history.

72

Conflict in Relations. In order to tackle an avalanche or an undertow, one must not fight it head on but rather slip or swim out of it sideways. Similarly, one must sidestep or take a step back in a conflict in a relation, where head-on collision may only lower the level of character on both sides. Stepping back must always remain an open possibility in relationships.

Un/familiar Relations

73

In Memory of Camus! Human life is full of absurd events and encounters. The fundamental challenge is to turn the absurd into an advantage, into a joy of life with which one can live.

74

Levels and Types of Disparity in Relations. We become unfriendly, or even hostile, toward acquaintances based on their apparent identity of associations without knowing their inner qualities. Such unfriendliness may remain unknown to the other person who may wonder why we keep a distance to them.

75

Nicety vs. Fairness! Those who always act nicely towards others do so as a defense mechanism against possible abuse that may harm them, mostly because they are unable to defend themselves. Therefore, nicety in their case is a sign of weakness. By contrast, fairness is a sign of strength, where fair people treat others with fairness as they expect to be treated as such. If not, they are ready to defend themselves and restitute fairness.

76

There is an uncanny, untouchable divide between the familiar and the unfamiliar in human relations; although these divides are not permanent, one may not force their change, lest one ends them entirely.

77

The Uncanny in Relations! At the libidinal root of the reasons as to why one could become friendly and sociable may lie precisely the very reasons as to why one would be repulsive. Most charming and cunning people, however, conceal their repulsive sides so that they could remain attractive.

78

There are different forms of gaze; many misunderstandings stem from misreading the other's gaze.

79

One cannot be more concerned for the goods and the people who are under someone else's care than those people themselves, lest that concern may induce shame.

80

Society benefits doubly from cohesive relations among its

members unlike societies that are stricken by divisiveness. Each form of divisiveness brings the society one notch down in terms of what it can achieve as a whole.

81

One loses power in public in proportion to the incriminating information others have on that person. Politicians often use such information to get ahead of their opponents. What is incriminating varies from public to public.

82

The nature of secrets one has, or the types of skeletons one has in one's closet, reveals the deepest aspects of one's character. These secrets, once revealed, could be damaging to the relations of that person.

83

No Angels or Saints! All humans have a dark side, pitiful, unpleasant, odious, hateful, disgusting, scary and awful... But no one wants to see it, no one wants to admit this psychological fact to themselves or others. The rational animals see themselves as true, good, and beautiful... so do they believe, so that they can live!

84

Painful Truths! There is a discrepancy in emotive response regarding one's own defects: if someone else tells us our defect to our face, we feel ashamed and upset; if we tell it to ourselves, we can brush it aside or deny it. And the shame deepens, if that someone else is not an intimate to us.

85

Endurance in Solitude! "Bare the pain of solitude longer and do not get in touch with that childhood friend" says an inner voice. But you do, you cannot endure your own self, your solitude. You build contact with former acquaintances whose life developments and goals you do not know. They may be in shabby business or suffering from character deficiency. You do not know any of that. Out of some old trust, you end up in shabby business with them. Now, your character is compromised. You could have listened to your inner voice and borne the pain of your solitude a tad more. Now you have to deal with your tarnished character.

Between the Familiar and the Unfamiliar

86

Intimacy and propinquity in relations expose character deficiencies that one would not otherwise detect in everyday life.

87

In dance one finds one's kindred spirit in free motion.

88

Love not Transmittable! Love is not a package that one can transmit from one loved one to the next. In traditional societies where customs bound people closely together, their members felt unified through a strong communal bond. If an elder loved two separate people, the assumption was that these two people would love each other. Such assumption of love erased the singularity of the person and ignored the differences among singulars. This is one reason why arranged marriages were common in traditional societies, whereas post-traditional societies frown upon them, and rightly so.

89

One must retain the uncanny in the other for that relationship to last. It must be remembered, but is often forgotten, that deep down we are all unfamiliar to each other; the pretension to familiarity is for security and self-preservation. The mysterious, the secretive and the unknown excite the relationship and sustain curiosity for one side to keep exploring what is hidden in the other.

90

The Dilemma of Transparency! It is difficult, nay, impossible to be fully transparent in a relationship, if one wants to sustain it. On the other hand, both sides of the relationship have to be on the same wavelength vis-à-vis transparency and what it entails. It so often happens that transparency leaves one side vulnerable at a given moment — hence, the impasse.

91

Levels and Degrees of Dissimulation! We often find ourselves in social milieus where we have to hide our true feelings and ideas from others, sometimes even our identity, so as to survive in those milieus; therefore, dissimulation is the first thing to do. Now, there are different types of milieus which necessitate different types of deception. The art of dissimulation is a sophisticated one; one has to know when, where, and how to dissimulate in the most effective and consistent way. Those who play this game cannot escape from the charge of hypocrisy, as Chamfort says: "It is dangerous for a philosopher who is in the service of one of the rich and powerful…to reveal his full disinterest. He would be taken literally. He must hide his true feelings, and he is, as one might say, one of nature's hyprocrites." (*Products of the Perfected Civilization*, p. 155). The context of Chamfort's maxim is one of the many types of dissimulations we engage in.

92

Self-interested Judgment! One names another 'angel' or 'devil' entirely based on one's own self-interest and regardless of this other person's inherent qualities. And I hear the objection coming: "But aren't all judgments self-interested?" I respond: "I grant that but insist on differentiating the self-interest." Again, we are back to the self and its varieties.

93

Unconscious Motives! There are always unconscious motives in every human relation. It is best, for the sake of healthy relationship, that some of these motives remain dormant.

94

What may be a character fault for one may not be so for another person. What one understands as character, and thereby character fault, depends on one's values, and not everyone has the same values.

95

The Demonic Gravity! Tendency to reduce the entirety of a human being to a single worst trait in that person, out of the many traits, stems from a deeply ingrained fear, namely, the fear of the monster within one's own self. To say it curtly, we demonize the other in order not to see the demon within.

96

Insidious Desire! Narcissists wish—but often do not express—that others not be narcissistic like them. Thus reigns their ego supreme; or, they would like it to be that way.

97

Rejected and Dejected! Those who are rejected by others can become excessively social in order to compensate for their past rejections and to preempt possible future rejections.

98

Diplomacy in Relations! One main challenge in human relations is to decline or reject someone's genuine proposal without necessarily offending or belittling them, especially when their proposal is an expression of their true desire.

99

Treating a stranger or an acquaintance in a familiar way in public, as though that person were a friend, could be a violation of his privacy.

100

Transgressing boundaries together with like-minded spirits is one thing, but not knowing one's boundary in relation to someone who is not receptive to that transgression is something else.

101

Allotments and Entitlements! For some, especially those in positions of power, the main attitude in human relationship is this: "You give me pleasure and I'll make you a king." Thus are many nobodies promoted to be somebody.

102

Give and Take-The Extent of Quid Pro Quo! The way one gives and takes reflects the nature of one's character. Some give with an abundance in their heart, some with strings attached. Some take the given and the giver for granted, others are grateful to what is given. Human life spans over the given and the taken, while transactional relations become detrimental.

103

Introverts and Extroverts!—no doubt, there is a spectrum in-between—become a burden on relations for different reasons: the former express very little and one never knows what they feel or want; the latter express too much and no one wants to pay attention to their demands any more.

104

The Ordinary vs. the Extra-ordinary! Depending on where one's place is in relation to the ordinary everyday life, whether one be a conformist or a rebel or in-between, one has a different perspective on life and human relations.

105

Strength and Weakness! One becomes strong to the degree of one's overturning of a harm or a damage done to one's self by others. In the absence of such transformation one remains weak in relation to that harm and to the one who did the harm.

106

Private vs. Public! In the public realm, humans are connected at superficial levels; in private, they have the possibility to bind at deeper levels. The danger in the latter, however, is when one runs into unreconcilable blocks, which can end that relation.

107

Private Facts / Public Information! Releasing information about someone's private life, unbeknownst and unwanted by that person, is a betrayal of trust and must be shunned, as long as that private information is not about any injustice against anyone.

108

Social and political structures of a society can modulate human relations up to a certain point, but cannot alter them from ground up. The spirit of law can go only so far.

109

Contra Capitalism .—. It is not only material poverty that can wreak havoc on human relations but also, and more importantly, the poverty of human character. On the other hand, too much wealth is often detrimental to character growth and can cause psycho-somatic disorders.

110

War and Peace on the Spectrum or the Bankruptcy of Warmongering and Peace-loving! Warmongers do not like the status quo and want to stir the pot without knowing what may come next. Peace lovers, on the other hand, want to preserve the status quo at all cost and would go as far as appeasing the warmonger to do so. And this may be their doom!

111

Intentions do not have much significance in relations when there is no one on the other side to "receive" those intentions.

112

One's intentions could be interpreted in a completely different way by others for whom the intentions were meant.

113

Laws of Physics! Attraction and repulsion among human beings work in mysterious ways. At the outset one may consider common interests, passions, etc. or reciprocal benefits. These, however, cannot fathom the complexity of human bonding. The different levels and intensities of energies shape relations more than people often recognize.

114

Faults of Memory! Humans have different capacities of memory whether of those of names or images, and their memories change as they age. In the aftermath of memory decline (not necessarily in dementia related old age disorders), it plays its own tricks. In one's accustomed environment, a stranger whom you think you never met may think that he knows you and greets you in a friendly manner. If you are also in image-memory decline, you may come to think that you know this stranger whom you think you never saw before. You fall into doubt, but you greet back out of politeness or the ambiguity of your remembrance. Similarly, with names: we remember the names we are accustomed to know, for instance, common names, and names that are unique, but forget those in-between. In short, our memories play unfathomable games with us, the likes of which we would not imagine when young.

115

The Return to the Unfamiliar! When relationships end, those of love or friendship, both sides start becoming unfamiliar to each other, as they were before they had met. To expedite this process of unfamiliarity, there is a common tendency to demonize the other, as one becomes ashamed of the relationship one had, forgetting that they once had many shared happy moments. As for love relations that end, La Rochefoucauld writes: "When two people have ceased to love, the memory that remains is almost always one of shame." (Maxims, §71).

116

Being Biased in Relations. Bias means harboring unfounded opinions about others and all humans have some bias about something or someone; what is crucial here is the degree and the depth of these biases and prejudices and how firmly one upholds them. It is clear that many biases impact human relations negatively; they prevent humans from having meaningful relations with each other. One question remains as to why people harbor biases, even when contrary evidence is clear, and how they spread. One explanation can be offered here; namely, that humans tend towards some 'agreement' so as to belong to society, which also connects with self-preservation. And the bigger the bias is, the bigger is its weight. On the other hand, one may not have the spirit of independence to stand up against the bias. Lastly, one may not have the courage to stand against the bias. In short, the herd is the fertile ground where biases flourish.

Techne, Technology and Relations

117

Techne. There are many words in many modern languages, which stem from the Greek word *techne*. What meant to be skill and crafting capabilities is now used for a variety of modern tools and tasks: technology, technician, technique, etc. To uncover its archaic sense, it is necessary to view 'techne' in a holistic way. There are different types of skills necessary for the life of an individual and society, not only professional skills in one's field but also social skills, among many others. One needs to be aware of this fact of culture and cultivate one's self as such.

118

Planetary Concerns and Reflections. How have advanced technologies of our age impacted human relations, among humans and also with other beings of this planet? How did humans end up destroying countless number of animals and plants even when they are not for direct consumption? Even the latter is not considered to be a sufficient excuse for such destruction. There is wisdom in "when one destroys other beings, one destroys one's self" and this applies to all beings. All beings are intra-beings or chiasmatic beings rather than pure beings. Purity is only an idea or for some an ideal; real purity does not exist. Those who recognize themselves as "intra-beings" have more possibility, plasticity and flexibility to be connected to other beings.

119

The dominant technological being-in-the-world can be reversed from instrumentality to intra-being enhancement. To that effect, old habits, customs, dispositions and ideologies must be transformed.

120

Instrumentalization of nature in modernity coupled with the crowning of the human as the highest and best being on this planet had dangerous and harmful impact; both are anthropocentric in their own ways.

121

With advanced technologies, sanctuaries for animals, not zoos or prison houses, must be created, where animals are untouched.

122

Digital technology and automated systems saved humans, to a some or large extent, from enduring the miserable aspects of the human condition. One does not have to put up with the crankiness and the misery of the drudge worker any more.

123

Internet and the social media have exacerbated the already existing forms of alienation — users dissimulate for harmful affects, as they hide behind their screens. Those who do not have courage for certain deeds now do them shamelessly and anonymously. Moreover, they have eroded the formalities in language, which are needed in the public realm so that its sanctity remains intact. Lastly, they amplified the crassness of the unformed masses. Those who are uncouth now display, more than ever, their lack of taste in public with no shame.

On Friendship

124

One cannot force a friend to be honest on matters concerning the nature of that friendship, lest it erupts an unrepairable bond.

125

The degree of one's honesty with a friend shows the proximity and intimacy of that friendship.

126

Complex characters can sustain complicated relations that overlap or crisscross with one another.

127

No le me tangere! "Do not pull me down with your expectations" says one side, but the other side does not heed. Unnecessary expectations exacerbate relations when one side imposes their way of living on the other side, instead of seeing the other side as a companion on life's journey.

128

Only complex types can upkeep different, sometimes colliding types of relations with the same persons. It is often said that friends cannot be business partners, or teachers cannot be friends with their students, or parent-child friendship is not possible. All of them show that one needs to be mature enough to have these multiple types of relations when the circumstances are ripe and when there is chemistry.

129

The inability to say 'no' in friendship, when one must say so, is the doom of that friendship; after that, it becomes a mere relationship.

130

Everyone has a private life the secrets of which cannot be divulged, even to friends.

131

It is wise not to share deep secrets with friends, if their divulgence will negatively impact that friendship.

132

Secrecy in Childhood. There is a dangerous type of being

private or keeping secrets from others, which stems from child's need to hide their forbidden or unwanted deeds from their parents. In all likelihood this may happen in strict parenthood milieu where the child's self-preservation weighs happily on the side of keeping secrets. The danger lies when this becomes a pattern and is carried into adulthood.

133

There is always a bubble of privacy among friends which should not be pricked. Once pricked, there may not be any friendship left.

134

Among friends, there is often a parity of emotions. This is not to say that friends feel or should feel the same emotion in the face of an event that they both experience. The parity at stake is not sameness but rather affinity and the absence of an object of negative emotion.

135

Spirits Close, Paths Apart! Two souls who were initially close and intimate but who traverse their own path of self-transformation may never meet again, not even at moments of respite; their paths may not ever crisscross, even though they are kindred spirits, once bound together.

136

Great spirits give signs to each other through erotic desire, even if their signs do not always find full receptivity. Nietzsche was in an unrequited love with Lou Salomé who later became Rilke's lover. Lou Salomé later became a companion of Freud in his psychoanalytic circles in Vienna, while Rilke became lovers with Madame Klossowski, the mother of Pierre and Balthazar Klossowski for whom he became a mentor. It was Rilke who introduced Pierre Klossowksi to André Gide. The erotic signs which first emanated from Nietzsche later spread through Gide and Klossowski brothers unto the erotic fields of the 20th century.

137

Judgment Day! Sometimes friends keep their deep secrets from each other in order to prevent them from making judgments about the implication of these secrets. In this way they can maintain their friendship undamaged. If the secret of one side is revealed, the other side would have to pass judgment, if not willingly, then under social pressure. Society demands that judgment day!

138

Simulation and Friendship. One cannot be fully transparent to others, including one's lovers and friends. Often times it is necessary to emulate a friend's feelings in order to sustain and retain the friendship. That one cannot be emphatic in every context should be obvious. In order to successfully emulate feelings that one does not feel authentically, one needs to use one's imagination like actors.

Sex in Relationships

139

The Art or the Science of Sexuality? Sexual activity reveals much about human character and relations. In it sexual partners' likes and dislikes, care and lack of care, sense of reciprocity or its absence, sensibility to pain and pleasure, tastes and distastes and many other qualities are revealed.

140

Not only one's sexual identity or preference, but more importantly, one's overall sexual practices reveal much about one's character, emotional make-up, perception of give and take, attitudes to care and relations to pain and pleasure.

141

Sexual desire can enhance human relations, and its expression and realization can build human character, as much as it can also ruin them. In what direction desire goes depends on the context, the desirous beings, their character and the affectivity in human relations. "Spiritualization of desire," to use Nietzsche's phrase, is the path to pursue for healthy relations of concupiscence.

Ancients and the Care of the Self and the Other

142

Contra Confucius. — One cannot respect one's superiors unconditionally. Such respect would deprive one of one's individuality.

143

The Double-edged Sword of Stoicism. — One would like to have a companion who is strong, has endurance, does not complain or collapse or give in at the slightest misfortune. This companion stands firm like an upright ship during a storm. This Stoic friend does not show or express any emotions either. One can say, all is fine; what else do you need? Well, it is the same friend who may harbor bitterness towards you, unbeknownst to you. You will never find out unless that bitterness explodes at an unexpected moment. And then your whole friendship is over.

144

Prudence for one's self cannot always be a goal, not for everyone, not in every context. This would erase all functions of expenditure.

145

Care for the public and the public good is a lofty Aristotelian and Confucian ideal, but the 'public' is not an undifferentiated entity. Therefore, one must ask oneself what in the public one must care for.

146

The boundary between care and control is shifty and shaky. It is often difficult to ascertain where care stops and control begins. Those in whom controlling others is a strong tendency aim to make others dependent on them; dependency is a means to control and gives excuse for it.

147

Fantasy vs. Memory! It so often happens that a fantasy created at a young age turns into the memory of an event that did not happen. The reverse could also occur, when a memory of an unpleasant event could be treated as a fantasy. Such are the tricks that the mind and the soul play on us.

148

Parents embellish fantasies about their children's early lives, which impact their memory and selfhood into adulthood.

These concocted stories, partly fictional, partly real, come to shape their level of narcissism and inferiority/superiority complexes.

On Bondage in Human Relations: The Herd and the Control

149

Formation of the Herd and Herd Mentality. Members of the society band together out of the necessity for self-preservation; otherwise, they would not survive alone. This fundamental aspect of human existence is the first necessity. The second necessity concerns the inclusion and avoidance of being an outcast apart from self-preservation. Humans are social beings and solitude is painful for them; as they evolved, it has become exponentially more difficult to survive alone. The third necessity is bound by what is expected to come as inheritance for the future, of title, wealth, power, etc. In short, many social factors pull the members of society into its vortex from which there is no ideological escape. The rest, what they say about who they are and what they do, is mere justification.

150

In tightly-knit social organisms, some elements try to control others; these social controls are often couched in intentions of well-being for the controlled parties whereas they are the manifestations of the power of the controlling party. In this hierarchical universe what is already powerful wants to maintain and expand itself and this happens through control.

151

Lilies in Marshes! One should not unequivocally expect to find only awful characters and relations in the worst repressive societies. Even there one can be surprised to find beautiful flowers. On the other hand, one often encounters many troubled souls in the so-called open societies.

152

When idiots rule a society, the bottom of the pot cracks up and all the nutcases fly into the open. When such nutcases determine the ruler, as in so-called democracies, the lid of the pot bursts open spreading vermin into the entire social body.

153

Every vision for a society has its presuppositions as to the nature of human relations in that society, if not concretely, at least at abstract levels. Every such vision has its high as well as low points.

On Ruling and Hierarchical Relations

154

How Does One Rule One's Own Self and its Relation to Ruling in General. It must all start with self-rule, a point often forgotten in politics and regimes of ruling (at micro or macro levels). First, one must know one's self and one's authentic needs and inclinations. Second, one must learn how to care for one's needs and drives. Listen to the life of your own drives, each one of them, and see what you hear. Then comes the mastery of drives; mastery does not mean control or suppression but rather nourishment, navigation, and channeling. There are contexts and arenas to satisfy all drives (which may not be always the case depending on one's society), even if some drives may take on substitute (Ersatz) objects. However, to come to this point of satisfaction of drives, many drive-actions are needed: one starves the drive or lets the drive loose and saturates it with excess so that one finds that medium in which the drive finds its home, so to speak. This experimentation is necessary so that the drive finds its "right" place. And every drive needs its own experimentation.

155

Now we have arrived at a place where all drives are satisfied and this type of self-ruling gains currency in that social collectivity. Since all selves are satisfied with themselves and with each other, let's remember that drive satisfaction does not take place solo but in its own community, all selves are attuned to one another to a large extent. There are now aligned communities based on drive-satisfaction. What needs to take place now is the coordination of these satisfied selves.

156

Collective Ruling 1. So far we did not speak of hierarchies; however, in the experimentation with drives, role models, guidance could be used, if they are available for those drives. It could be so that such models do not exist. In any case, we have benefited from role models and they have become our teachers in our self-ruling. They have not imposed their way of life on us, but rather stood as examples above us. That is already a hierarchy, a hierarchy that pushes us further and higher, rather than repressing us.

157

Collective Ruling 2. Some of us have mastered their drives better and they are better connected socially. They are better connected internally but also connected externally, as they understand their diverse needs and the diversity of their own collective whole. These will be the ones who are suited to coordinate all the satisfied selves and drives. They will be on top of this "natural" hierarchy. This exceeds discussions on single vs. multiple rulers.

158

The forms of affectivity, which authority figures use in any political structure, cannot be confined only to two emotions such as fear and love, as Machiavelli suggested. There is a broad range of emotions that emerge from top to bottom, emotions of envy, anger, hate, revenge, etc. Whichever emotions are more dominant and how they come to be in this way shape those political structures and their affectivity.

159

The desire to prove that one is always right, even when wrong, outside the context of the courts, is a sign of insecurity. One appeals to logic to do so and does not consider the possibility of a variety of positions on the same subject.

160

When one is established as an authority figure, one then feels obliged to be always right. Otherwise, such people sense a loss of authority, when they believe they are not right.

161

Authority is enmeshed in a network of different types of human relations from security and dependence to trust and mutual benefit, to name a few.

Needs, Needs and Needs...

162

Human beings are the neediest beings on earth, because their needs are often inflated.

163

Those who do not know what their needs are blame others for not having their needs fulfilled.

164

Needs are both physical and cultural; more often than not, they are hard to separate.

165

The use of an object cannot be assessed solely on the ground of physical need. This would erase the fact that human beings are cultural/spiritual beings.

166

Needs can be inculcated into someone artificially, creating in them a need for something they do not truly need.

167

Marx's distinction between "exchange value" and "use value" is useful to some extent; ultimately, knowing what one really needs is a function of culture and value.

168

Much of human relations revolve around fulfilment of needs whether they be physical, developmental, emotional, social or cultural.

169

All drives need their fulfillment; it is possible, however, that some drives remain 'happily' dormant in human relations.

170

Relations are based on the fulfillment of the needs of some drives.

171

It is impossible to fulfill the demands of all drives in one relationship.

172

Drives and their needs must concur for both sides to be content in a relationship.

On Silence in Relations

173

It is not time but silence that heals.

174

The Manifold of Silence or the Elevator Syndrome. Silence manifests itself in many different forms. First, one may speak of immediate vs. mediated silence. In the former, the silent one is in the same space with others; silence is used in a variety of ways. One has nothing to say or does not or cannot say what should be said or is afraid of speaking or cannot find the most fitting words to utter or cannot speak due to overwhelming emotions. Here it is space that determines the nature of silence. In the other kind, the mediated silence, the silent partner is not in the same place with the object or the addressee of silence. It could be a friend who remains silent, when a gesture, for instance, a call, is expected from the friend. This type of silence is conditioned by time, the time that is endured in the space of that relationship. Perhaps the friend will break the silence and speak from a distance, but it has not happened yet. And the silence continues...

175

Secretive in Silence. There is a dangerous, harmful type of being private and keeping secrets from others, which stems from children's need to hide their forbidden deeds from their parents. In all likelihood, this may happen in the milieu of strict parenthood where the child's self-preservation weighs heavily on the side of keeping secrets. This unconscious habit becomes a burden when it turns into a pattern and is carried unto adulthood.

Language in Relations

176

Ultracrepidarians and Flibbertigibbets burden human relations with their nonsense talk. One must know when to talk and when to remain silent, but this exceeds their capability.

177

Human speech has been abused for so long since its inception in early humanity and it still is.

178

Consensus vs. Con-spirituality! It is not consensus but rather affinity of spirits which should shape and dominate human relations. The former is based on the model of linguistic communication, while the latter on the symbiosis of kindred spirits.

179

On the Psychology of the Loquacious. Why do some people talk too much—and "talking too much" is from the standpoint of the recipient. Since human character types are diverse, there cannot be one explanation of this social phenomenon. This existential fact, however, should not stop one from reflecting.

It could be that they have too much to say but cannot express them concisely, or concise expression is not their strength. Or, that they have to show that they know. Or, that they are carried away with the passion of their subject matter. Or, they cannot read the cues from the others who are listening that their talk has extended too far and no one is listening any more. Ultimately, the loquacious people may not be in touch with others, as much as they are not in touch with themselves.

After-Thoughts on the Staircase

180

If this is the only life one has, one then has to invest in relations that are meaningful to oneself and the other. Or else, one lives in the vicious circle of miserable relations.

181

Nothing is Permanent! If necessary, one must end a toxic relation for the health of one's soul and mind. And for the health of the other as well.

182

Stains of the Soul! When a first stain is smeared on someone, it is difficult to remove it. If a second one follows, it becomes impossible.

183

The body reveals many signs regarding the nature of a relationship. If one is uncomfortable or in distress with someone, then the body feels awkward and out of place; one sees twitches, contortions, agitated movements, shaking legs, eye contact evasion and many other signs that emanate from the body in discontent.

184

Do not tell me what you lived! One cannot convey the insight of a lived experience to other humans unless they had a similar experience. Our genuine communications are based on parallel lived experiences, even if they happen in different places and times.

185

Humanity will take one step forward when it abolishes the family institution that promotes nepotism based on familial bonds and when humans learn how to treat the unfamiliar as familiar and vice versa.

Last Stop on this Aphoristic Route

186

Needless to say but better said, human relations are often wrought with difficulties. It is more difficult to handle those relations that are close and intimate, as in family or work relations. One cannot end those relations easily. These relations become more painful when they include abuses, or the needs of those in those relations are not met, or someone is treated unfairly or unjustly. They become even more painful when such mistreatments are not acknowledged. In short, it is difficult to be *human*…

187

Human relations can be worked on the way one works on one's own self. The former is difficult because the sides may not concur on how they want to work on their relation.

188

Those who are introspective and insightful about themselves and others would be willing to listen to the other side, if the other side is willing to talk. But it is a rare occurrence that all those who are in the same relation would be introspective. Most humans seek their own self-interest and believe to be on the right side even if they are wrong. In such cases, no dialogue is possible and the problems of their relations persist. Again, it is difficult to be human…

189

Someone in a difficult relationship has enough and wants to open up a dialogue; why can't we sit down and talk about our problems? They start talking and turn in circles because they are both right and no one wants to take a step back. They cannot break out of the vicious cycle; perhaps they need an outsider who can help them break that cycle. But they do not believe in such outside interference. They are back to where they started.

190

No Causality! It is difficult, nay impossible, to make inferences of causation in human relations. In other words, one cannot say this happened because of such and such, since one cannot know the inner lives of the people implicated in such inferences. At most, such speculations would miss their insightful target.

191

At the end, one may have enough with this sarcasm on being human and screams: why don't you go to your cave and live like a hermit? Why are you in relations with humans? Go live with your plants and animals and let's see if you can live a life of contentment in the wilderness. You are a writer with no skills to survive in nature. You may not last even a few days. If it is difficult to be human, it may be even more difficult to be non-human, especially when you have been a human for so long.

192

And the hermit replies: Even if I go back to my cave, I will still be human. I cannot take the human out of me. I utter these words as a warning to humans not because I resent being human. Don't take me for a misanthrope; if I were, I would not be writing these words of admonition. Take care of your/self and work on your relations; you are here only once.

193

Often silence is the best cure: Let's remain silent for a while….

A Short Bibliography

Adorno, Teodor. *Minima Moralia*: Reflections from Damaged Life, tr. by E. F. N. Jephcott, New York: Verso, 1974.

Bataille, George. *Guilty*, tr. by S. Kendall, Albany: SUNY Press, 2011.

Chamfort, Nicolas. *Products of the Perfected Civilization*, ed. by W. S. Mervin, New York: Norton Point Press, 1984.

Cioran, Emil. *Tears and Saints*, tr. by Ilinca Zarifopol-Johnston, Chicago: University of Chicago Press, 1995.

Darwin, Charles. *The Expression of the Emotions in Man and Animals*, New York: Penguin Classics, 2009.

Fontenelle, Bernard de. *Dialogues of the Dead*, tr. by Lord Lyttleton, London: Cassell & Company, 1889.

Gracián, Baltasar. *The Art of Worldly Wisdom*, tr. by Joseph Jacobs, New York: Frederick Ungar Publishing Co., 1892.

Heidegger, Martin. *Being and Time*, tr. by J. Stambaugh, Albany: SUNY Press, 2010.

Joubert, Joseph. *The Notebooks of Joseph Joubert*, tr. by Paul Auster, New York: New York Review Books, 1983.

Kafka, Franz. *The Zürau Aphrorisms*, tr. by Roberto Calasso, New York: Schocken Books, 2006.

Kilpatrick, David. *95 Theses on the Reformation of Football*, Beadle Books, 2022.

Kierkegaard, Søren. *Philosophical Fragments*, E. H. Hong, Princeton: Princeton University Press, 1985.

La Bruyère, Jean. *Characters*, tr. by J. Stewart, New York: Penguin Classics, 1970.

La Rochefoucauld, François. *Maxims,* tr. by Leonard Tancock, New York, Penguin Books, 1959.

Lichtenberg, Georg. *The Waste Books*, tr. by R. J. Hollingdale, New York: New York Review Books, 2000.

Nietzsche, Friedrich. *Human All-Too-Human*, tr. by R. J. Hollingdale, Cambridge: Cambridge University Press, 1986.

Pascal, Blaise. *Pensées*, tr. by A. J. Krailsheimer, New York: Penguin Classics, 1995.

Rée, Paul. *Basic Writings*, tr. by R. Small, Chicago: University of Illinois Press, 2003.

Schlegel, Friedrich. *Philosophical Fragments*, tr. P. Firchow, by Minneapolis: University of Minnesota Press, 1991.

Schopenhauer, Arthur. *The Wisdom of Life and Counsels and Maxims*, tr. by Bailey Saunders, Amherst, NY: Prometheus Books, 1995.

Spinoza, Baruch. *Ethics*, tr. by E. Curley, New York: Penguin Classics, 2005.

Steinmann, Michael. *Painfully Clear: Aphorisms on the Problem of Happiness*, New Jersey, 2024.

Vauvenargues, Luc de Clapiers. *The Reflections and Maxims of Luc de Clapiers Vauvenargues*, translated by F. G. Stevens, London: H. Milford, 1940.

Also by Yunus Tuncel

Complete Fragments: Notebook A (Authors House, 2008)

Towards a Genealogy of Spectacle (Eye Corner Press, 2011)

Agon in Nietzsche (Marquette University Press, 2013)

Emotion in Sports (Routledge, 2019)

Nietzsche on Human Emotions (Schwabe, 2021)

Flames of Passion: Towards a Genealogy of Feeling-Notebook F (Beadle Books, 2022)

Nietzsche, Gai Saber and Modernity (Transnational Press of London, 2024)

The Devil Gave the Poison to Eros: Notebook E-Eroticism (Beadle Books, 2024)

The editor of *Nietzsche and Transhumanism* (Cambridge Scholars Publishing, 2017)

One of the co-editors of *Nietzsche and Music* (Cambridge Scholars Publishing, 2022)

The Editor-in-Chief of *The Agonist*

www.ingramcontent.com/pod-product-compliance
Lightning Source LLC
Chambersburg PA
CBHW060340080526
44584CB00013B/848